A Picture Puzzle Book

Look & See
Michigan
With Me

By Kathy-jo and Ed Wargin

We would like to thank the Mackinac State Historic Parks

for allowing us to photograph Fort Michilimackinac,

The Henry Ford Greenfield Village in Dearborn, Michigan

for allowing us to photograph the Farris Windmill, and

the Ketvertis family of the Pumpkin Barn in Levering, Michigan

for the wonderful hospitality, pumpkins, and harvest fun.

Most of all, we thank Jake Wargin for his assistance

(and perpetual sunshine) throughout this book.

Sleeping Bear Press

310 North Main Street, Suite 300
Chelsea, MI 48118
www.sleepingbearpress.com

THOMSON

GALE

© 2007 Thomson Gale, a part of the Thomson Corporation.
Thomson, Star Logo and Sleeping Bear Press are trademarks
and Gale is a registered trademark used herein under license.

Printed and bound in Canada.

First Edition

10 9 8 7 6 5 4 3 2 1

Library of Congress Cataloging-in-Publication Data on File
ISBN: 978-1-58536-323-0

Look & See Michigan with Me is a picture puzzle book that encourages the reader to compare pictures and actively seek the changes from one scene to the next. Traveling through Michigan with lighthouses and beaches, Detroit cars, forts, and flowers, to a Michigan extravaganza with all of our Michigan favorites, there are hints and clues in the poems to help readers begin finding changes. **Look & See Michigan with Me** is a fun and interactive way for friends, families, and readers young and old to "Look and See" together, talking about the changes they find and how many wonderful things there are to see and do in Michigan.

Look & See with Me *hint:* I'm looking for beach balls and towels that flip.
Michigan beaches are summer's best trip!
I'm looking for changes in water, on land.
I see smiling faces that sit on the sand.

Look & See with Me *hint:* Mackinac Island where canons are booming
is perfectly pretty when lilacs are blooming.
I look for the horses that walk through the streets
and bicycles riding past arches and treats!

Find
15
Changes

Look & See with Me *hint:* I'm looking for bobbers
in lakes fresh and clean.
It's Michigan fishing
that sets up this scene.

The stringers keep changing.
See lures new and old.
Keep counting the numbers
of hooks shiny gold.

Find
23
Changes

Look & See with Me *hint:* I see a windmill that's lovely and old.
It sits in a village where stories are told.
Now look for new changes that turn in the sky,
count windows and pathways of days now gone by.

Find
16
Changes

Look & See with Me *hint:* I see paddles and sticks,
and quick-flying tricks
as I look from the lake to the sky.
I see lessons in riding, quietly gliding,
and daring new ways to fly.

Find
19
Changes

Look & See with Me *hint:* Detroit Motor City assembles the ride.
History shines and it's our point of pride.
I'm looking at cars, and trucks with a load.
To find every change keep your eyes on the road!

Find
25
Changes

Look & See with Me *hint:* I look for lost items from time long before,
a dusty old barrel, a flag, and a door.
I look for a tower to see old with new.
Bridges and buildings will change with the view.

Look & See with Me *hint:* I see flowers in bloom from the south to the north
as Michigan nature is blossoming forth.
Tulips and trillium that catch every eye
while little red goodness is baked in a pie.

Find
10
Changes

Look & See with Me *hint:* I'm looking for teams that say Michigan sports
with jerseys for baseball and basketball shorts.
Look close for each player, each banner, and ball.
The numbers keep changing, can you find them all?

Find
21
Changes

Look & See with Me *hint:* I'm looking through windows and seeing the light,
of Michigan beacons that flash through the night.
Chimneys and changes, some big and some small,
some will trade places, can you spot them all?

Look & See with Me *hint:* I see bright colored pumpkins, a wagon to ride,
a barn with a window to see what's inside.
The wheels on the tractor are keeping in line
when you look for the harvest, watch every sign!

Find
18
Changes

Look & See with Me *hint:* I see the sails in the sky billow white.
Michigan boating is one fresh delight.
I look for the changes in ways that we row.
A boat speeds away while the others go slow.

Look & See with Me *hint:* I see the mitten; it's filled with the best
of Michigan favorites from east to west.
I see the boaters and bikes on a trail,
a musical place, and a ride on the rail.

I see the apples and robins that peep,
castles and symbols and fresh ways to sleep.
From snowshoes to sunshine, to ships at the docks
look north to south and see Michigan Rocks!

Find
31
Changes

About the Pictures:

With more than 3,200 miles of shoreline, the most freshwater coast in the nation, there are many wonderful sandy beaches to explore, making Michigan a well-visited destination for summer tourists. There are **sixteen** changes in this set, many of them small and tricky. You have to keep your eye on the ball to find all of these!

Mackinac Island is located in the Straits of Mackinac, a strip of water separating Lakes Huron and Michigan, as well as the lower and upper peninsulas of Michigan. A popular Michigan tourist destination where motorized travel is not allowed, most people enjoy the island by horse and buggy, bicycle, or foot. There are **fifteen** changes in this set.

Fishing is a popular pastime in Michigan, and with more than 11,000 inland lakes and four Great Lakes, there are many opportunities for anglers on inland lakes to seek fish such as walleye and largemouth bass, while those who fish on the Great Lakes can attempt to catch salmon and steelhead fish. Can you look at the map and point out where your favorite inland lake should be? There are **twenty-three** changes in this set; did you find them all?

The Farris windmill is believed to be the oldest windmill in the United States, and is located at Greenfield Village at the Henry Ford museum in Dearborn, Michigan. Built in the mid-1600s and used for grinding corn, it operated in three locations in Cape Cod, Massachusetts before being brought to Michigan. The Henry Ford is the nation's largest indoor/outdoor museum, showcasing America's historic past as well as the people and ideas that have changed our lives. There are **sixteen** changes in this setting.

There are many ways to have fun in Michigan, as well as **nineteen** changes in this set. With lakes, forests, ski resorts and more, there is always an opportunity to enjoy the outdoors. In Michigan you are never more than thirty minutes away from a Michigan State Park, State Forest Campground, State Recreation Area or Trail System.

Detroit is the Motor City, and known as the automobile manufacturing center of the world. In 1908 Henry Ford introduced an automobile called the Model T, and it did not take long for this moderately priced vehicle to create a new age in personal transportation and "motor touring." Henry Ford also introduced the moving assembly line, which revolutionized the automobile production industry, making it easier and more cost-effective to build cars. There are **twenty-five** changes here. Can you identify the types of American cars you see here? How have cars changed through the years? How might they change in the future?

Fort Michilimackinac was originally built by the French along the south shore of the Straits of Mackinac in approximately the year 1715. Its original purpose was to serve as a supply trading post for French traders working in the western Great Lakes region. In 1761 the British gained control of the fort and continued its use as a trading post, but in 1781 abandoned the fort and moved to Fort Mackinac on Mackinac Island. With so many historic elements in place, from windows to guard towers, it is a step back in time to find the **fifteen** changes here. How many historic forts do we have in Michigan?

Native Americans were Michigan's first farmers, planting items such as corn, beans, and squash. Today Michigan is still a farming favorite, and is a leading producer of goods such as beans, tart cherries, blueberries, corn, and soybeans. There are more than 50,000 farms in Michigan, nearly all of which are family owned. In the autumn, many family farms and orchards open their doors and become a fun place to enjoy hayrides, pick pumpkins and apples, and learn a bit about our tradition of Michigan family farms. There are **eighteen** changes in this set. Can you find each one?

There are **fifteen** changes in this boating set. Did you find them all? Keep your eye on the changing sails and small details of each scene. With more than 7,000 miles of streams for canoeing and kayaking, and more than 11,000 inland lakes and four Great Lakes, there is a place for every type of boat. Can you name each type of boat you see here? How many other types can you list?

There are **thirty-one** changes in this scene filled with Michigan favorites. You will find special state symbols such as the robin, an apple blossom, and white-tailed deer, and symbols of favorite things such as biking along trails, beaches, camping, and boating. From the northern reaches of the Upper Peninsula to the metropolitan area of southern Michigan, our state is filled with a rich history of tradition and innovation, opportunity for education as well as unmatched natural beauty along its and in its wilderness. As the heart of the Great Lakes, Michigan is a place of nature and culture, and among this map you will find m in the items that represent some of the special features of M

of flow official state e trillium is a our forests each me the other flowers? e considered orchids?

Team sports have a long and rich tradition in Michigan. There are many professional sports teams in Michigan such as the Detroit Red Wings hockey team, Detroit Lions football team, Detroit Pistons basketball team, Grand Rapids Griffins hockey team, and the Detroit Tigers baseball team, to name a few. College team sports also inspire many dedicated fans as well as rivalries, one of the biggest being Michigan State University versus the University of Michigan football teams. Women's sports have a long tradition in Michigan too, and as far back as the late 1800s some high schools had women's basketball teams. There are **twenty-one** changes in this scene; can you find them all?

With more lighthouses than any other state in the nation, Michigan is a popular lighthouse-seeking destination. Lighthouses come in different shapes and sizes such as schoolhouse shape, square, conical, and cylindrical. Although many Michigan lighthouses still remain under federal authority, numerous lighthouses have been sold to private individuals or organizations dedicated to preserving the architecture of these special structures. There are **twenty-three** changes in this set, but they are difficult! If you look closely at the small and important details of each lighthouse you will find them all!

Ed Wargin is
known for his beautiful image
Michigan Notable Book Award wit
A Robert Traver Legacy: Legends of
as well as the newly released L
Au

There are **ten** changes in this set of flowers. The apple blossom is the official state flower of Michigan, and the trillium is a favorite sight to see in our forests each spring. Can you name the other flowers? Which ones are considered orchids?

Native Americans were Michigan's first farmers, planting items such as corn, beans, and squash. Today Michigan is still a farming favorite, and is a leading producer of goods such as beans, tart cherries, blueberries, corn, and soybeans. There are more than 50,000 farms in Michigan, nearly all of which are family owned. In the autumn, many family farms and orchards open their doors and become a fun place to enjoy hayrides, pick pumpkins and apples, and learn a bit about our tradition of Michigan family farms. There are **eighteen** changes in this set. Can you find each one?

Team sports have a long and rich tradition in Michigan. There are many professional sports teams in Michigan such as the Detroit Red Wings hockey team, Detroit Lions football team, Detroit Pistons basketball team, Grand Rapids Griffins hockey team, and the Detroit Tigers baseball team, to name a few. College team sports also inspire many dedicated fans as well as rivalries, one of the biggest being Michigan State University versus the University of Michigan football teams. Women's sports have a long tradition in Michigan too, and as far back as the late 1800s some high schools had women's basketball teams. There are **twenty-one** changes in this scene; can you find them all?

There are **fifteen** changes in this boating set. Did you find them all? Keep your eye on the changing sails and small details of each scene. With more than 7,000 miles of streams for canoeing and kayaking, and more than 11,000 inland lakes and four Great Lakes, there is a place for every type of boat. Can you name each type of boat you see here? How many other types can you list?

With more lighthouses than any other state in the nation, Michigan is a popular lighthouse-seeking destination. Lighthouses come in different shapes and sizes such as schoolhouse shape, square, conical, and cylindrical. Although many Michigan lighthouses still remain under federal authority, numerous lighthouses have been sold to private individuals or organizations dedicated to preserving the architecture of these special structures. There are **twenty-three** changes in this set, but they are difficult! If you look closely at the small and important details of each lighthouse you will find them all!

There are **thirty-one** changes in this scene filled with Michigan favorites. You will find special state symbols such as the robin, an apple blossom, and white-tailed deer, and symbols of favorite things such as biking along trails, beaches, camping, and boating. From the northern reaches of the Upper Peninsula to the metropolitan area of southern Michigan, our state is filled with a rich history of tradition and innovation, opportunity for education as well as unmatched natural beauty along its shores and in its wilderness. As the heart of the Great Lakes, Michigan is a unique place of nature and culture, and among this map you will find many changes in the items that represent some of the special features of Michigan. Enjoy!

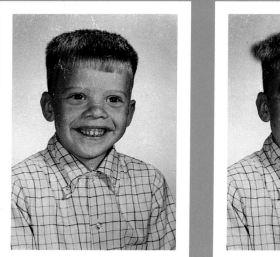

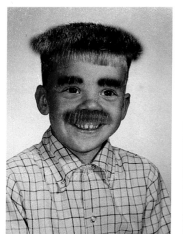

Ed Wargin is an award-winning landscape photographer well-known for his beautiful images from the Great Lakes region, including Michigan Notable Book Award winning books titled *Voelker's Pond, A Robert Traver Legacy; Legends of Light, A Michigan Lighthouse Portfolio;* as well as the newly released *Lake Michigan, A Photographic Portfolio*.

Author *Kathy-jo Wargin* is the best-selling author of more than twenty-five books, including *The Legend of Sleeping Bear, The Legend of Mackinac Island,* and *The Michigan Reader*. Although the couple has worked jointly on coffee-table books such as *The Great Lakes Cottage Book* and *Michigan, The Spirit of the Land,* this is their first collaborative children's book, inspired and created by their mission to encourage children to notice the small details in the beauty that surrounds them everyday.